The Embrace of the Soul

The Embrace of the Soul

Reflections on the Song of Songs

Charles Rich

Edited, with an Introduction by
Ronda Chervin

ST. BEDE'S PUBLICATIONS
Still River, Massachusetts

Censor deputatus   Raphael Simon, OCSO

Imprimatur   +Timothy J. Harrington
Bishop of Worcester

February 6, 1984

Acknowledgments

Excerpts from the Song of Songs are taken from the *New American Bible*, copyright © 1970, by the Confraternity of Christian Doctrine, Washington, D.C., and are used by permission of copyright owner. All rights reserved.

Cover photograph: Detail from *The Life of Christ*, "The Last Supper," portfolio of ten wood panels by Ivan Mestrovic. Published by Syracuse University Press, 1952. Used with permission.

LIBRARY OF CONGRESS CATALOGING IN PUBLICATION DATA

Rich, Charles.
   The embrace of the soul.

   Includes bibliographical references.
   1. Bible. O.T. Song of Solomon—Criticism, interpretation, etc.   I. Chervin, Ronda.   II. Title.
BS1485.2.R53   1984   223'.906   83-23066
ISBN 0-932506-31-3

Contents

Foreword

I first met Charles Rich about forty-five years ago when I was a psychiatrist in New York City and he was living much the same life as he has lived since, a life devoted to prayer and works of charity. We both were converts from Judaism, Charles having entered the Church a few years before I did. I shall return to the subject of our friendship towards the end of this Foreword.

As Dr. Chervin indicates in her sensitive Introduction, a strong current of contemporary biblical exegesis regards the Song of Songs as an erotic love poem; by some as describing human love in relation to monogamy and conjugal fidelity: "for love is stronger than death," as the Song says.

It is quite true that human love is set forth unashamedly in this Song in terms of two lovers praising and extolling each other's beauty. Such indeed was and still is the practice in the Near East, where love songs abound at the seven day feast of marriage. Of these songs, the Song of Songs is the most outstanding.

Sex is God's image stamped on man and woman and sexual union is the consummation of a love which mirrors the divine love in its totalness, exclusiveness and demand for utter fidelity.

Is there strong reason for sensing a deeper meaning in this Song? Does Scripture itself give us any clear indications?

The Hebrew prophets Amos, Isaiah, Ezekiel, Jeremiah, Hosea find human love and marriage to be the most apt way of expressing the relationship of Yahweh to his people, and through them this usage is found throughout the Jewish Bible.

For the Christian Fathers this marital relationship is fulfilled between Christ and his Church as well as between Christ and the individual person. This explains the presence of this Song in both the Jewish Bible and the Church's Scripture.

The Cistercian Fathers—particularly St. Bernard, William of St. Thierry his friend, and Gilbert of Hoyland his disciple—delighted in finding in the Song a very apt means of describing the human and divine interrelationship. For them as for the Hebrew prophets, no better one could be found in and through which to reveal what takes place between the human and the divine lovers. It is in this tradition that Charles Rich's work falls, as Dr. Chervin remarks.

In his seventieth sermon on the Song of Songs, St. Bernard says: "Holy love is the only object treated in this Song. We must remember that love reveals itself, not by words or phrases, but by action and experience. It is love which speaks here, and if anyone wishes to understand it, let him first love. Otherwise it would be folly to read this song of love, because it is absolutely impossible for a cold heart to grasp the meaning of language which is so inflamed."

But is such love only for a select few? Says Bernard: "Those who have not yet enjoyed such an experience should ardently desire it. We do not hesitate boldly to proclaim that every soul, if it is vigilant and careful in the practice of all the virtues, can arrive at this holy repose and enjoy the embraces of the Bridegroom" (Sermon 46:5; 57:4, 11).

Is such love self-centered, selfish? We will touch on Charles Rich's spirituality in a moment. Bernard answers for him in these words: "The love which is contemplation is God's own loving in the soul, and such love cannot exist in the soul when she resists its movement towards the needs of others."

Two friends attuned to each other by a long intimate friendship in which they share their lives, aspirations, intentions, and work, have a privileged capacity to understand each other, despite differences in background, education, and culture. So it is with those attuned to the Holy Spirit by a long intimate relation with Jesus Christ in which his life, aspirations, intentions, and work have been shared.

It is this which gave Bernard his insights into the Song of Songs, and it is this same rich sharing in the Spirit of Jesus Christ which gives Charles Rich the insights he offers us in this book. Here are two hearts resonate as one. Thence comes the authenticity of doctrine, the outpourings of love, the wisdom of the Spirit which encourage us to go forward in the way of love.

Here there is an inwardness shared freely, which incites our love—and is not such incitement the Father's purpose in revealing to us his Son, in sharing him with us truly in the Eucharist, in showering upon us his Spirit and incorporating us in his Church?

To this purpose I can testify that Charles has been beautifully faithful in the forty-five years I have known him—relishing God in love, drawing others into that love—sure-footed because of the completeness of his surrender in love to Christ, including the full acceptance of his teaching known to us through the Church, its teaching authority, its Scripture, Fathers, Doctors, and Saints.

Indeed it was my appreciation of Charles' fidelity to the Spirit which in the first years of our friendship led to my Cistercian vocation forty-three years ago, when Charles encouraged me to visit the community which I joined and to which I still belong.

In my experience, Charles has always been a man of wisdom, of humility, of obedience and of love. His has been an unconditional obedience to the teaching and discipline of the Church, a characteristic of all the saints and of all those who make progress in the discipleship of Christ. This led him to a contemplative union with Christ such as those who attempt to attain it without the discipline of obedience of mind and heart, or through sheer humanly-induced "emptiness of mind" cannot dream. Hence too he has been gifted by the word of the Spirit through which he has guided and still guides, enlightens, encourages, and consoles many in one-to-one contact, as well as through his writings.

The reader is invited to step into Charles' circle and with him to offer himself or herself to the Spirit, open to his influence within while reading words that come directly from a heart which is so closely united to the heart of Christ.

Charles is just as direct in his day-to-day life as in his writing, and perhaps a couple of anecdotes will best illustrate this. In one of my first contacts with Charles, adverting to the fact that he had had an ulcer, I said to him in the mid-afternoon, "Would you like a glass of milk, Charles?" His response was, "Now let's get this straight, we talk about God and only about God!"

Forty years later, Charles, as he got into a car with his friend and a Brother from St. Joseph's Abbey to visit St. Benedict's Priory in Still River, said: "In this car, we speak only of God!"

To friends who have offered to pay his complete expenses for a six week trip to the shrines of Europe and to Rome, or a ten day trip to Mexico City, Charles has declined saying, "I find in God all the pleasures you find in these trips. I pray for you, and you should be glad that I refuse to go, otherwise you might have reason to question the genuineness of my life of prayer!"

Charles' life is an incentive and encouragement to us, but needless to say we do not have to model ourselves on his manner of speaking and acting, but rather to pursue just as uncompromisingly the graces of our particular vocation. The basic conditions for discipleship are the same for all, as Vatican Council II has pointed out, in insisting that all are called to the same holiness.

May the fire which burns in Charles' heart enkindle the world!

Raphael Simon, OCSO
Spencer, Massachusetts

Introduction

These reflections on the Song of Songs are the work of Charles Rich, a lay contemplative living in a Jesuit House.

In Charles Rich's first book *Reflections from an Inner Eye*,[1] there can be found a description of his long search for Christ culminating in his conversion fifty years ago. Rich came from a Chasidic Jewish background. As a young boy he spent hours in the forests of Hungary in meditation. When the family came to America, however, he found it hard to capture the spirit of prayer amidst the chaos of the Jewish ghetto.

Gradually he lost his faith, but never stopped searching for truth wherever he thought he could find it. For years he studied the writings of philosophers, poets, novelists, and religious men in the hope of finding some kind of salvation.

It was only after a very unusual religious experience in a Catholic Church that Charles came to believe that Jesus Christ was truly divine. Once a baptized member of the Mystical Body of Christ, the natural mysticism which had sustained him during the long years of despair blossomed out into a classical contemplative life not unlike that of

his favorite saints, Teresa of Avila and John of the
Cross. After a time of solitary living in poverty,
his Jesuit director found a place for him as a
layman devoted to prayer within a Jesuit residence.

The few hours of his day not rapt in contemplation were spent in the study of the lives and
writings of the saints. In particular he was
attracted to the great commentaries on the Scriptures by the Fathers of the Church.

The writings on the Song of Songs, the Canticle of Canticles, were particularly inspiring to
this Jewish Christian convert.

Steeped in the allegorical interpretation of
the Song from his reading of the Fathers, it was
natural that when he came to write his own
reflections on the Canticle they should be in the
same vein.

The allegorical interpretation of the Song of
Songs as a depiction of the love of the soul for
God and of God for the human person or the
Church, is not, of course, the only way of reading
the Song. Some prefer the literal meaning.
Others study the literal meaning in order to
derive from it a basis for the morality of court-
ship and marriage.[2] In such cases, the possible
analogies in the poem to the human/divine relationship may be considered to be somewhat
secondary, or even implausible.

This editor, being a philosopher and spiritual
writer rather than a theologian, is in no position
to resolve the controversy about the best way to

interpret the Song of Songs. Instead, I will simply include here some of the reasons given by Charles Rich for choosing to follow the traditional Jewish and Christian allegorical method.

He writes that prior to the Christian era, the Jewish people interpreted the sensual images of the Song in a purely allegorical manner. We have indisputable proof of this in what is now known as the "Targums" to the Old Testament writings.

The Catholic Church adopted the interpretation given to the Song by the ancient synagogue with this exception: where they used the word "Synagogue" she substituted the term "Church," and where the name of Israel occurs, we speak of the members of the Mystical Body of Christ.

The ancient rabbis held that the Song of Songs was one of the greatest gifts of God to the human race. "The whole world was not worth the day on which this Song was given to the people of Israel," are the words of the famous Rabbi Akiba.

However, the Song was not given to everyone to read. It was only for those who through prayer and meditation had overcome their sensuality so that there would be no moral danger to them in immersing themselves in the lush imagery of the Canticle.

It should be remembered that the Jewish writers of the Bible took a mystical approach to life. For this reason, the language they made use of was figurative and symbolic. Semites did not use abstract terminology, but preferred to make their love for God known by concrete analogies.

To this day the Jewish people pay special homage and reverence to the Song by making use of it in their liturgical prayer.

It is natural to assume that Our Lord, Jesus Christ, was harking back to the beloved Song of Solomon when he spoke of himself as the bridegroom and his followers as the bride (Mt. 9:15; 25:1-13; Mk. 2:19-20; Lk. 5:34-35; Jn. 3:29).

The early Christian commentators on the Canticle such as St. Athanasius, St. Hippolytus, Origen, Gregory of Nyssa, and, most eloquently, St. Gregory the Great and St. Bernard, followed the Jewish tradition of interpreting the poem as an allegory of divine love.

Later mystics in the Church always took special joy in the words of the Canticle, for these provided some kind of expression for their own ecstatic experience of the beauty of God.

Here is a wonderful passage by St. Teresa of Avila, a doctor of the Church, concerning the aptness of this analogy to divine love: "You may think," she says to her nuns, "that in these canticles there are some things which might have been said in a different way.

"We are so stupid that I should not be surprised if you did. I have heard some people say that they actually tried not to listen to them. O God, what miserable creatures we are! We are like poisonous things that turn all they eat into poison. The Lord grants us great favors by showing us the good things which come to the soul that loves him by encouraging it till it can hold converse with his Majesty and delight in him; yet from these favors we derive only fears and we attribute meanings to them which sort well with the little love we feel for God" (*Conceptions of the Love of God*).[3]

To come to an end of this introduction, I will add that because Charles Rich's reflections were written in prayer in a spontaneous way, it has been my task as editor to reorganize the insights under various headings.

The first chapter will be about the allegorical beauty of the Song, and speaks about the place of allegory in the spiritual life. The next three will deal with general themes in the Song: the yearning for eternity, the love of Christ, and the rapturous joy of union with God. Then will follow meditations on each of the lines of the sacred poem which the author chose to comment on.

May the Holy Spirit open our minds and hearts that we may enter into new regions of the Kingdom as we read on.

Notes

[1]*Reflections from an Inner Eye* (No. 11 Plaza, Huntington, Indiana: 1976).

[2]See the interesting study by Pouget and Guitton, *The Canticle of Canticles*, trans. Joseph L. Lilly (The Declan X. McMullen Company, Inc., 1946).

[3]*The Complete Works of St. Teresa of Jesus*, Vol. 1, trans. and edited by E. Allison Peers, (NY: Sheed and Ward, 1957).

From The Song Of Songs

Let him kiss me with the kisses of his mouth...
  Your name spoken is a spreading perfume...
Tell me, you whom my heart loves,
  where you pasture your flock,
where you give them rest at midday,
    Lest I be found wandering
  after the flocks of your companions...
Ah, you are beautiful, my beloved,
  ah, you are beautiful...
    Our couch, too, is verdant...
I delight to rest in his shadow,
  and his fruit is sweet to my mouth...
He brings me into his banquet hall,
    and his emblem over me is love...
  Strengthen me with raisin cakes,
    refresh me with apples,
  for I am faint with love...
Hark! my lover—he comes,
  springing across the mountains,
    leaping across the hills...
My lover stands behind our wall,
  gazing through the windows,
    peering through the lattices...
My lover speaks: he says to me, 'arise, my beloved,
  my beautiful one,
    and come! For see
    the winter is past,
    the rains are over and gone.

The flowers appear on the earth;
   and the song of the dove
      is heard in our land'...
My dove, hiding in the clefts of the rock...
Let me see you, let me hear your voice,
   for your voice is sweet,
      and you are lovely...
   My lover belongs to me, and I to him...
On my bed at night, I sought him
   whom my heart loves.
   I sought him, but I did not find him.
I will rise then and go about the city,
   In the streets and crossings
I will seek him whom my heart loves.
   I sought him but I did not find him...
The watchmen came upon me as they made
   their rounds of the city:
      Have you seen him whom my heart loves?...
Let my lover come to his garden
   to eat its choice fruits...
      I was sleeping, but my heart kept vigil...
Open to me, my sister, my love,
   my dove, my perfect one...
Set me as a seal on your heart, as a seal on your arm;
   For stern as death is love,
relentless as the nether world is devotion;
   its flames are a blazing fire.
Deep waters cannot quench love,
   nor floods sweep it away.
Be swift, my lover,
   like a gazelle or a young stag
      on the mountain of spices!

Allegorical Beauty of the Song

On earth the joys of eternity are veiled in figures of speech which sound obscure and enigmatic. In the life to come, the full flush of them will inundate the soul and carry it into that "somewhere" for which we can now find no adequate expression. All we can say in this respect is that somewhere Christ himself dwells in all his glory.

The Song of Songs deals with the ecstatic love the soul has for Christ and which he has for the soul. There is an interchange of graces and blessings and this is in the Song called "kisses of the mouth" signifying immersion in God's essence.

Loving God as the favored person does, she naturally desires to give expression to this love. In doing so she gives utterance to words that sound strange to those in whom this love is not present. It is for this reason the Song is so little understood, if not misunderstood. St. Paul says we have to become fools for the sake of Christ.

The Song of Songs makes use of concrete terms to describe what is spiritual. What we shall one day experience in the life to come is hinted at in images. In that exalted existence we shall comprehend in a spiritual manner what we are not able to know in a physical way.

How infinitely kind and good God is to have divinely inspired the writer of this Song to recreate our hearts with words so beautiful to read, reflect and meditate upon and this with all the fervor and diligence of which we are capable.

"How sweet to my palate are your promises sweeter than honey to my mouth" (Ps. 119:103) the psalmist says. The words of God are indeed pleasant to read and meditate upon by those who have the grace to extract from them the sweetness from heaven they all contain.

In the Song of Songs God wishes to recreate our hearts with his own beauty, as that beauty is made manifest in the person of his Son. God loves us so much that this must be made manifest to us. He outdoes himself, so to speak, in the Song in trying to make his love penetrate the depths of our inner being. There is a fascination about the words of the Song of Songs, attracting to themselves minds and hearts which have been purified by faith.

There is nothing written with more power than the Canticle of Canticles to soothe the heart of man and to distill into it the balm from heaven for which all the prophets longed prior to the coming of Christ into this world.

The Song of Songs speaks of this balm, but it does so in words that signify the good things of this earth. In words of earth the Song speaks of what we will one day find when we get to heaven and not before then. Why not on earth? As shall

be explained at length in a later section, because
all finite beings fail to fulfill their promise of total
unending joy.

We love the Song for its depiction of our homeland in eternity, expressed in such beautiful
figures of speech. Yet unless we are pure of
heart, we will never succeed in discerning in its
words what the Holy Spirit intends; the Spirit
who loves us with such ardor and intensity. The
Song of Songs speaks of what is too sublime for
unrefined natures, unrefined and not yet purified by the grace of the Most High God. Carnal-
minded men and women will find nothing in this
Song but what their lower natures crave. They
will miss its purely divine import. They will not
see in this poem what all the saints perceived in it.

"I will destroy the wisdom of the wise, and
thwart the cleverness of the clever," (1 Cor. 1:19)
the Spirit says in upholding all that has a divine
origin and so can only be discerned in a supernatural way.

The saints were not ashamed of the language
made use of by the Spirit in the Song of Songs.
Those who are not saints, however, are scandalized by the bold and daring way in which God
addresses us and we him.

It is the will of God that for us to learn what he
is like, we should have recourse to himself.
"Learn from God about God" was the motto of all
the saints and doctors of the Church. With this
principle before us, it is to different portions of

Sacred Scripture we should turn in order to attain a living experience of the beauty of the divine nature which took on our mortal flesh and became man for our sake. It is in the Song that we come to a sense of the beauty of God-made-man mirroring the attribute of beauty in God the Father.

We have need of beauty in our lives, for it is by its means heaven discloses its sweet and sublime secrets to the soul of man. We cannot live in a vacuum, and so out of the goodness of his divine heart, Our Lord has seen fit to fill this vacuum for us.

In certain portions of Scripture we pay homage to the goodness of God, to his wisdom, power, and justice. But here in the Song of Songs, it is the inexpressible beauty of the God-Man which strikes us so forcibly and becomes the source of so much genuine joy and consolation.

See how beautiful he is whom we love so much. This seems to be the burden of the Song. In the history of the Church, we know that many saints died of love. They were entranced by the beauty of Christ's being. In the Song of Solomon, he whom we so love is not depicted as a teacher, or a reformer, but as the lover par excellence.

This is why we cannot penetrate too deeply into what the Holy Spirit is trying to communicate to us by means of its strange and startling language. St. Thomas of Villanova said of this Song that it was the "most difficult and sublime of the whole of Scripture." The more we study its words the more clearly do we perceive the truth of this saint's remark.

We have many necessities as we journey through this life, and Sacred Scripture, like a medicine chest, has a remedy for every earthly ill. As we find ourselves approaching the metaphorical gates of eternal life, we find in ourselves an even greater need than before to transcend intellectual knowledge by a more poetic sense of Christ's presence. How many die interiorily because of a lack of such a vibrant spirituality. Without it, they cannot be united with their Father in heaven.

In the Song we transcend the ordinary approach to our divine Lord. Body and soul become the medium through which the Son of God has chosen to manifest himself.

It is the aim of our Father in heaven to instill into our souls truths and insights into himself which he knows would be a source of delight to us. But due to our present imperfect status, God cannot do this save by figures of speech and symbols of what causes us joy in a physical way. We have need to be raised up to the divine heights of bliss on which the Godhead dwells, and so in order that this may be accomplished, we are spoken to in the terms found in the Song of Songs such as kisses, fruits, flowers, and the parts of the human body.

In one of his sermons on the Song, St. Bernard

tells us that to have a living experience of what God is like, we have to have devotion to the humanity of Christ. It is by means of this humanity that God reveals himself to us in a way consistent with our mortal nature.

"Let sweetness," this doctor of the Church says to us, "be overcome by sweetness." By "sweetness" he here means Christ's flesh, the love of which acts as a kind of charm preventing the soul from completely giving herself over to what passes away with time. In everything it has to say the Song of Songs makes mystical reference to the flesh of Christ, though it does so in figurative terms.

Unless we ask God to "heavenize" our lives, we cannot fully appreciate the Song. To love God in the right way we have to live on earth as if we were no longer upon it. At least, we must do so in the higher part of our nature.

If ever there was an age which needed Christ, it is the one in which we at present find ourselves. It has need of the God-Man as he is depicted for us in the Song. How ardent, intense and passionate are the earthly strains of music with which this Canticle speaks of him who shall constitute our unending joy throughout all eternity.

The words of God carry in their wake meanings that are infinite in extent. They are not meant to be understood merely intellectually, but felt inwardly and this in a way we cannot articulate by words of any kind. When we read the

Song we feel ourselves drawn into the kind of world they are in who are now in heaven. There are secrets of love in the words of this Song which will be made manifest to us after we shall have left this world.

In the same treatise of St. Teresa, *Conceptions of the Love of God,* quoted earlier, she tells the nuns she was directing not "to be surprised at the tender words which you may read in the Scripture as passing between God and the soul." It is God who loves us and he does so in a divine way. How can the creature hope to fully understand the Incomprehensible One our divine Lord is? Certainly the expressions made use of in the Song of Songs are startling and mysterious. They are sensuous to a remarkable degree, and so unless we deeply spiritualize ourselves we will fail to perceive their mystical import and attribute to them meanings not intended by the Holy Spirit. For as long as this world shall last, devout and learned men and women will go on making holy commentaries on the Song of Songs.

Earth is a place of exile from the Lord. For this reason the Psalmist has written that he could not "sing the Song of the Lord" in the foreign country, which this life will always be for those who love God to excess (Ps. 137).

Soon we shall die, and when we do we shall carry the thoughts of this Song with us into the next life. What greater grace is there than to have its words in our hearts as we are about to emigrate from this world? After a lifetime of love for God and of servce of him, with what rapturous delight the reading of the Canticle fills the minds and hearts of believers of the true faith. What is there which is too great a price to pay in order to obtain a deeper insight into its many beautiful themes?

The Yearning for Eternity in the Song of Songs

Christ is the "desired of all nations," since it was for the beauty of the God-Man all the nations yearned and longed. This yearning is expressed in the masterpieces of Greek sculpture, philosophy, and drama. Our whole life on this earth is comprised in longing ardently and passionately for what God has willed should not be found upon it. It was for this reason the Jews of old were known as "pilgrims."

Our English poet, William Shakespeare, has a character in the play Anthony and Cleopatra say, "I have in me immortal longings." Every Christian can repeat these words as part and parcel of the religion which he/she practices, since it is for eternity such a person lives and not for the sake of a few paltry years. It is these very longings for immortality which distinguish us from the rest of mankind.

The world is sick with the sickness time brings about. We stand in need of that divine physician, Christ, to enable us to acquire health of soul. The body is good, but that which transcends it, the soul, is of infinitely greater worth. And so, when we read the Song and reflect on its profound mystical truths we are borne upwards into the

Kingdom of our Father in heaven, into which we shall be brought one day by the grace of Christ.

There is Christ himself in all his glory. How blessed are the dead for being where we ourselves hope to be. We do not so much wish to die as to see Jesus in his unveiled presence. With the great Apostle, "we groan while we are here, even as we yearn to have our heavenly habitation envelop us." While we live in our present tent we groan; we are weighed down because we do not wish to be stripped naked but rather to have the heavenly dwelling envelop us, so that what is mortal may be absorbed by Life. God has fashioned us for this very thing and has given us the Spirit as a pledge (2 Cor. 5:2-5).

Out of his infinite goodness and love, God keeps us in this world until it becomes absolutely clear to us that what we are looking for cannot be found in it. In the Song of Songs Our Lord is spoken of in a way and manner which renders the beauty of his being irresistible. In it, the soul is beckoned to take flight to the heights of his divinity since it is there alone that all its God-instilled cravings can be appeased. "Be swift, my lover" (Song 8:14), God says to all such. "Make haste my beloved," God says to us every single moment of the day and night, indicating in these words that it is his will we should long for him exclusively.

No merely earthly joy is able to satisfy our craving for the transcendent Good, Truth, and Beauty of Jesus. "Vanity of vanities," says Qoheleth, "vanity of vanities! All things are vanity" (Eccl. 1:1). "Vanity of vanities," this author says as regards everything that can be experienced in the present life. Is it then any wonder that he should speak to us in the Song of Songs the way he does? Christ is the "mountain of spices," since in him is embodied such goodness.

Not science, not art, no particular human being, dear and precious as that person may be, no one but Christ should become the center of our lives, the root and fundament of all we are and hope for in this life. No one but he alone is able to satisfy the needs of our God-given nature, since he alone is the beginning and end of everything for which we yearn and hope for in an intense and passionate way. The Song of Songs presents this truth symbolically by means of images of delight in the beloved. It is for this reason we love it so much and expend so much prayer and study on all it has to say.

"By the rivers of Babylon we sat and wept when we remembered Sion" (Ps. 137:1). The rivers of Babylon constitute our present mortal state. We sing this song because of the realization we have that we cannot go back to the state of bliss whence we came save by the way thereto that Christ alone is. Has he not himself said to us: "I am the Way"?

Christ is the path we have to tread, leading us to himself. And so, unless we do so, we shall never find the kind of joys for which we have been created—infinite and everlasting ones, which sinners cannot have because they turn away from them.

"There is a way there," the prophet says, "and it shall be called the Holy Way: the unclean shall not pass over it" (Is. 35:8). Throughout the Scriptures, the Spirit speaks of the "way" to God which is a life of holiness. So unless this way is trodden by us, we shall not find him.

The Song of Songs deals with love alone, and as we draw close to our home in heaven, love becomes the criterion we apply to all things pertaining to our spiritual life. There is a beautiful expression in the writings of St. John of the Cross: "At eventide, you will be examined by love alone." We cannot go to heaven unless we love him who constitutes the happiness we shall there have. Read aright, in the Christian context, the words of the Song of Songs will give us a living experience of what the joys of the life to come will be like.

Centuries ago, at the time the chosen people were dispersed into captivity among the nations, one of their prophets gave utterance to the words: "Is there no balm in Gilead, no physician there?" (Jer. 8:22). Among the ancients, this balm was a kind of balsam used for the healing of wounds, and so, spiritually speaking, the author may have had in view the wounds of sin which Christ the Lord came to heal by means of grace. There most certainly is balm in Gilead and it consists in the coming of the Saviour into the world, since in him we have henceforth a means of healing the soul of the many abberations brought upon it by means of the devil's instigations.

Though we today are in a fundamentally different historical position than the one of the chosen people, in a deeply spiritual and mystical way these words of Jeremiah have a relevance as well for the Christian man and woman of our present-day world.

We, too, in the midst of our innumerable evils and distresses can say with the Prophet: "Is there no balm in Gilead? Is there no physician there?" And the answer which will be given us by an infinitely loving and merciful God will be: "This is my beloved Son. My favor rests on him" (Mt. 3:17). Christ is the balm in Gilead for whom the prophet longed and so it is to him we have to go to have the wounds of our souls healed from sin. In the Song of Songs these wounds of ours are healed by means of his love. This love is so divine that it makes us feel that our sufferings have never been.

We love Christ on earth so that we may do so in heaven. It is there alone that we will really enjoy having known him all the time we have been on this earth. The life we are now in is a kind of rehearsal for the existence we will have there. We love the Son because he speaks to us of this bliss for which no name can be found, since "eye has not seen, nor ear heard, nor has it entered the heart to conceive" all we will there have and enjoy with the same kind of happiness the angels themselves experience.

There is a need in ourselves for the kind of delight they experience who are no longer in this life. We have been told by Our Lord that we shall be as "gods." We need something too sublime for our thought to comprehend. It is this need the Song of Songs is meant by God to fill.

To understand all the Song has to say, we stand in need of God's grace, since without this grace, the words in it make no sense. Without this grace they even shock and scandalize us. Song of Songs, we should say to ourselves, how fortunate we are to be able to extract from your words what the Holy Spirit intended we should derive from them!

God wants us in heaven, and so it is for this reason he allows things on earth to be what they are and does not restore them to the paradisiacal state in which Adam was before he sinned. It is for this reason St. Augustine tells us not to promise ourselves what Christ did not promise us, freedom from suffering and pain of every kind on earth. "Earth," a saint said, "is not the Christian's home. Let those who want it, have the earth" (St. Realino, SJ). When we read the Song we have, so to speak, to get off the earth. When we read the Song of Songs, our hearts are lifted up to heaven and we rejoice at the realization of what is there awaiting us. "If there is one thing," a saint said, "that has the power to sweeten the tedium of life it is the haunting desire to depart from it."

As we go on living, we think more and more of eternity and less and less of time. We then think of the eternity of love Our Lord is, and of this same love the Song speaks in such beautiful imagery, the imagery of flowers and perfume, and the sweet odors of a mystical kind which they inhale into themselves who have been raised up to the transforming union of the God-Man, who sums up in his blessed person infinitely more than we could ever conceive or imagine.

Sweetness seems to be the essence of the Song of Songs. When it speaks to us of Christ, it seems to emphasize the divine sweetness of his wondrous nature, this wondrous nature of his consisting in the fact that he is both God and Man at the same time. There is a need in man to express the inexpressible, the inexpressible good and beauty Our Lord is. We should let ourselves become entranced by him who is more precious to us than the entire universe. We should let the Christ of the Song captivate our hearts. With the saints we sing, "Song of Songs, Song of love, Song of Christ," redeem and sanctify us.

"Deep calls unto deep," we hear the Psalmist say. These words of his remind us that there is something in ourselves which Christ alone can satisfy. Christ is God and so the satisfactions he brings to the soul have about them the atmos-

phere of divinity and endlessness. The Song is a
sort of window through which we can see all that
is waiting for us in eternity.

We must live for the eternity of joy that Christ
is or we will find ourselves in a position in which
nothing we do and are will have any meaning. We
must live the kind of life Christ came to bring,
there being none other worthy of an intelligent
human being. "Come, Lord Jesus." The saints
were always thinking of their home in heaven. It
was this meditation that was responsible for the
beautiful way in which they lived.

We have been made for heaven. It is because
we believe this that we are Catholics. Without
this belief in heaven there would be no point in
calling ourselves followers of Christ—for he is in
heaven. There is a movement afoot to disparage
belief in the life to come and to make this earth
the center of our hopes and activities. The devil is
jealous of our faith in the joys of heaven, so he
does all allowed him by God to discourage men
from thinking about these joys, that our hearts
may be as miserable as his own. The devil hates
the hope we have of our one day being with God.
There are gloomy people in the world today who
tell us not to think of the next life. They do this
because they are unknowingly performing the
devil's will. The devil hates holy and inspiring
thoughts so he does all he can to steal them from
our hearts. When we hear anyone saying to us
that we should not think of heaven we should

consider such a person an enemy to what is deepest in ourselves, that for which the Son of God lay down his precious life. Our Lord died so that we could have the hope one day of being with him in the paradise of his beatific state. By reciting the Song of Songs and meditating on its profound mystical meaning, we frustrate the devil's evil designs and bring his efforts to nought.

When we die we lose everything and we gain everything. From the enjoyment of what is created, we pass to the uncreated delight laid up for us from all eternity. Let us think of heaven all the time and dwell, in the Spirit, on the joys that are there waiting for us.

The Love of Christ in the Song of Songs

Those entranced by the love of Christ will never cease to have the words of the Song of Songs in the depths of themselves. We cannot love God too much and neither are we able to praise his divine Son adequately. The Song manifests the ecstatic love the soul has for Christ and which he has for the soul. Christ is the only solution to the problems of this life—Christ in the form of love as depicted in the Song.

When we open the pages of the Song of Songs we feel ourselves raised up into another world, one which is fundamentally different from the one we find ourselves in most of the time. The world of the Song is one of love and of love only. It does not deal with the ordinary aspects of Christian life but with that in it which is extraordinary, for which one has to prepare oneself by a life of virtue. That is why the Rabbis of old held that "the whole world was not worth the day on which this Song was given to the people of Israel."

The Song of Songs is the favorite Song of all the saints. The nearer they draw to their home in heaven the more ardent and intense their love for it becomes. At the end of our lives we will experience the kind of love which St. John the Evangelist says that God himself is. In the Song one thing only is asked of God by us who love him: "let him kiss me with the kisses of his mouth." As long as we stay in this life, we cannot have Christ in all his fullness. We cannot serve two masters, and these two masters consist of created and uncreated good things.

If we are sad in this life and depressed by it, this is due to the fact that we have not centered the whole love of our hearts upon him who alone is worthy of that love and who, because he is both God and Man, can never fail in the requital of it. Human beings are good. Now and then they have the power to make us happy. However, the happiness we derive from loving things God has made has about it a merely provisionary nature. It is for this reason all the saints set their standards above the things of time and rooted them in eternity. We cannot live in a vacuum. We have to love and having to love, why not love the Love Itself Christ is?

We cannot love adequately in the present life. It is only in the life to come that we will worthily love all we now find lovable. There is a defect in everything since the Fall and so it cannot be cherished and esteemed without qualification. Christ constitutes the only unqualified love, and so he alone is able to satisfy the craving in our souls for what is infinite and transcendent. We have been created with a capacity for endless delight. Creatures are able to satisfy us to a certain extent but after awhile they begin to pall.

In everything that the Song of Songs says it symbolically affirms and re-affirms that earth is not the place to love, but heaven. And so we wait for that "Day of the Lord" when we shall at last satisfy the God-implanted instinct in ourselves for perfect love. It is for this reason it has been written, "happy now are the dead who die in the Lord" (Rev. 14:13). They alone have attained the kind of happiness and well-being for which God made us. We have been made by love and for love and so nothing but love is the end we have in view. "My son, give me your heart" (Prv. 23:26).

"I have loved you with an everlasting love" (Jer. 31:3). Who but the Everlasting One is able to say these words to us? How often does not the creature promise what is in the province of the Creator alone to be able to bestow? All that creatures can do is to hint at the good God alone is able to be for us. Love him, they say, by whose bounty we are what we are. Ours, they exclaim, is a borrowed beauty belonging to him who is beauty itself. By means of the creatures, we are attracted to him by whom they have been made.

We love others as we do our own selves. But we love him by whom all these have been made in a higher way. Someday this being that is the outer part of ourselves will be taken away. All that will be left is that portion of ourselves which we will take with us to heaven. The saints never failed to recognize that there are two parts—or tendencies—to a person: one of earth, the other of heaven. As we go on living and accumulating the wisdom that Christ gives, it is the heavenly part of ourselves that occupies us and not the lower, earthly one. It is the aim of the Song of Songs to emphasize this higher part of our nature and to minimize the practical part. In the higher stages of the spiritual life there is neither rhyme nor reason. There love alone is present, enrapturing the soul with intoxicating delight.

From the moment of our entry into this world until our last breath, everything that God either wills or allows to happen to us is motivated by nothing else but his infinite love. Love alone accounts for the many vicissitudes it is his holy will should take place in our lives. Even the great and incomprehensible mystery of the sufferings we go through is a manifestation of God's love for us. When we get to heaven we will fully realize how everything we found so difficult to bear in this life was but another way of God saying to us how much we have been loved by him.

The great Italian poet, Dante, wrote as the last words of the *Divine Comedy*, "The love that moves the sun and the other stars," (*Paradiso*, Canto XXXIII, 140). God is love and so everything that takes place in the universe has this love for its motivation.

From the cradle to the grave God never ceases to manifest to us how deeply we are loved by him.

The saints saw God's holy will in everything he allowed to take place in their lives, even in the most trying circumstances. We have to look for the signs of love in everything connected with our earthly days. Then at the end of our life's journey we will be given the grace to say to Our Lord the words of the Song of Songs.

God wants us for himself. It is this which accounts for all we have to go through in this life. The Lord thy God is a jealous God, we are told in the Old Testament. Because he wants all the love in our hearts, God permits events to take place in our lives which will make certain that these hearts of ours will, in the long run, belong completely to him alone.

The spiritual life consists, to a great extent, in waiting for the coming of Christ in all his majesty and glory. How weary we become of this life when we think of heaven and all that is there awaiting us! Few people, though, find themselves supernaturally weary of this existence. That is because it is few to whom heaven is so real and vivid that the thought of it is constantly in their hearts. It is the sweet words of the Song which can make heaven vivid to us. Once in heaven we shall not fear, we shall not hope, nor will there be any need of the exercise of faith, for we shall see what we believe.

Sanctity consists in being in love with Christ and remaining so until the last breath of our earthly life. It is unthinkable to live without the love of Our Lord, and this both in time and in eternity.

"Love never ends...for our knowledge is imperfect; but when the perfect comes, the imperfect will pass away. So faith, hope, love abide, these three; but the greatest of these is love" (1 Cor. 13:8-13). So wrote St. Paul in one of the most amazing passages of his letters.

"We love thee, O Christ, and we bless thee, because by thy holy cross thou hast redeemed the world."

The Rapturous Joy in the Song of Songs

There can be no greater punishment than to be a stranger to the kind of joys described in the Song, joys we shall only fully experience when we get to heaven.

To really love God as he wishes we should love him, our divine Lord has to enrapture our hearts and minds so that we can be transformed. It is characteristic of the world to "go its own sweet way," but it is also characteristic of him we love so much to go his own sweet way, the sweet way of heaven.

When Adam and Eve were in Paradise, they experienced some of the joys described in the Song of Songs, divine and supernatural ones. There is a joy from heaven they alone know who are pure of heart. All throughout Scripture that purity of heart Our Lord spoke of when he came on earth is praised.

The Song of Songs represents the soul's Sabbath rest in Christ, a rest which begins on earth and continues throughout eternity. This "Sabbath" signifies the contemplative state wherein the beauty of Christ brings with it the kind of repose enjoyed by those who already see him face to face in the world to come. There is a word in Hebrew for this kind of rest which brings with it every imaginable and inconceivable good. Those who possess this rest, or "shalom," have need of nothing more to make them everlastingly happy and well off. In the contemplative state which those in heaven already enjoy, Christ is experienced in the way and manner of which this Song speaks.

There is a passage in the Book of Revelation which reads: "I heard a voice from heaven say to me: write this down: happy now are the dead who die in the Lord! Yes, they shall find rest from their labors, for their good works accompany them" (Rev. 14:13). What these labors are is not specified, but one may conjecture that they consist in the effort that all the saints made during their lives to get to know Christ better by means of their increased knowledge of him so that they would be able to love and serve him in a more worthy manner.

How many intensely long for the beauty of Christ without ever so much as suspecting that it is he they long for. How many there are who go to their graves without having even for one moment tasted the beauty of Christ's being! It is in this their sad lot lies.

It is the exact opposite with the saints. Having had the grace to know Christ by personal experience, they have no doubt of the infinite joys awaiting them after this life is over.

The world envies the saints for their having known God in a deeply intimate way, like to that of those already in heaven. We must ask for the grace to love the love of Christ, for without that love, this whole life is nothing but an unending naught.

In the Song of Songs we are given a foretaste of all we shall one day enjoy in heaven. Figuratively and mystically, all its joys are described there. By means of this Song we can re-enter paradise, so as to partake of the delights that were there before sin was committed. For a Christian, heaven begins on earth and paradise can be located in his/her inmost self, there where Our Lord said he will take up his blessed abode.

This is the meaning of the words of the Lord when he said, through the mouth of St. John, "Here I stand, knocking at the door. If anyone hears me calling and opens the door, I will enter his house and have supper with him, and he with me" (Rev. 3:20). Our Lord here referred to that divine food in the form of his mystical doctrines which the bride-soul said was "sweet to her taste."

The souls who love Christ sing their way into paradise, that place of delight which we regain as soon as we close our eyes in death. We cannot live without the music from heaven the Song of Songs plays in so enigmatic and mystical a way.

Heaven is the solution to the problems we have on earth, and heaven only. When the trouble we have becomes too much for us to bear, we have to immerse ourselves in the joys that are waiting for us upon our departure from this life, since this is the only way our earthly existence can be borne with the proper amount of Christian composure.

Life upon earth is a "warfare," we are told in the Book of Job, and so we have to have the weapons which our faith in a future life supplies in order not to be overcome and defeated in this encounter. As long as we live we cannot fight off the enemies of our souls without the armor supplied by the Christian religion. Those who will not make use of these arms will go down in defeat.

"Faith means battles," St. Ambrose tells us. Unless we wage warfare with the weapons of faith, hope, and love, we shall be conquered by the enemy of the human race, namely, the devil. It is he who does all allowed him by God to prevent us from believing in the joys of the future life. It is these joys that are the Christian's legitimate goal and not any other kind.

Many are looking for solutions to the problems of this life without ever realizing that these solutions can be found in Christ alone. "False is the salvation of men," the Psalmist tells us. But how few there are who pay any attention to what he has to say. It is otherwise with the saints. They have the grace to take the words of God literally, so the problems they have are not those of other men and women who are not as holy as they, and as loving.

There is a war within us and it takes place between what is higher and what is lower in our human make-up. This is the "good fight" of which St. Paul speaks. Everyone must wage it in an uncompromising way. As long as we shall live, there will never be complete peace within ourselves. That which is above will always be engaged in mortal combat with that which is below, the worldly part fighting the spiritual, without any let-up. In this respect, we often say, "peace, peace, where there is no peace." There is no peace in that part of ourselves which is in constant rebellion with what is higher in ourselves. Because of the warfare that will always go on between these two parts of our nature, Our Lord proclaimed that he was bringing a sword and not peace.

There is, of course, a peace which is consonant with our love for all Our Lord stands for. But the possession of this kind of peace can only be had by continual warfare with that in ourselves dragging us down to the level of those who are eternally lost. Spiritually as well as physically, we cannot live in this world without being exposed to dangers of every kind. Realizing this is the case, we ask God for the grace to protect us from these evils.

In order not to be laid low by what is inferior in ourselves, we have to continually aim at the heights of truth and beauty that are Jesus. And though there are dark moments in our lives, and dismal ones, we have to think of the times when we were free from them, and that these times will in due course return again. When dark and depressing thoughts do all they can to make entry into our souls, we must fight them off with the knowledge of all that Jesus is and what he has done for us by means of his passion and death.

Christ is joy, beauty, and love multiplied to an infinite degree. It is upon Christ we call when we find ourselves depressed in spirit. Has he not been called the Medicine of Life? O Lord and Saviour, how we must rally round the divine love you are in order to render the troubles of this life bearable to ourselves! How frequently the need arises in our lives when we must say, "Lord, to whom shall we go, for you have the words of eternal life." Where but in him can be had the balm from heaven for which all the prophets sighed? At such moments how consoling it is to read the words of the Song of Songs, since it is in them we will find that for which pure hearts yearn.

We must become saints, for otherwise this life will withhold its many secrets from us, and thus we shall not attain to the stature of the God-Man. The God-Man is the ideal around whom we must center all the love of our human hearts. When we do so, we shall receive on earth a goodly taste of what the joys of heaven are like. The joy of the saints consists in the realization they have of God being present in all existing things. Without his presence in them, they would not be. The saints knew that no matter what we may do, we cannot flee from the divine good Jesus is. "Love if you can," St. Augustine wrote, "anything that God has not made."

No matter what we may do, we cannot get away from God. It is in this realization that our whole happiness lies. Even the sins we commit, providing these are not of a grave nature, cannot separate us from him who is spoken of in the Scriptures as he who always is. Christ is everywhere. He is especially present in the souls of those who have the good fortune to be able to believe in him. When we move among men and women, the realization comes over us that, do as we may, we actually mingle with him by whose goodness and love these men and these women have been brought into existence. With this in mind, there is a necessity not only to get back to God, but also to become by grace what he himself is.

What a dreary world this would be without the Son of God in it! We cannot even imagine such a world, since without him, it would not exist. We are told in the Gospel of St. John that "in the beginning was the Word." Christ is the beginning mentioned in the Book of Genesis. In and through him, the world was created and without him there would be no world.

How unhappy they must be who lack the light, the interior illumination of the soul, which our divine Lord was meant by God to be. By light the Jews of old meant inner brightness of spirit, a kind of spiritual delight known and experienced by all the saints.

We need the inner brightness of soul that Christ is; and without which light we are in the darkness of which the prophet Job spoke when he said: "Perish the day on which I was born, the night when they said the child is a boy! May that day be darkness...may darkness and gloom claim it..." (Job 1:3-5).

We need the inner joy which the Christian religion imparts to the souls of all true believers, since without that joy there would be within us the dark pessimism of the pagans. We need the joy and delight of the Song of Songs, since without it we end up in an atmosphere of gloom like that of unbelievers.

We need joy in our lives as a torch which enables us to see the horizons of another and infinitely more beautiful life than the present one. If God were to give us the whole world of material riches and withhold from us belief in his divine Son, where would we be? Would we not be where they had been prior to the Incarnation? By "they" we mean the pagans of the Greek and Roman nations.

We need the lightness of heart and the joy of mind faith in Christ brings with it, as this faith is so entrancingly shadowed forth in the word-music of the Song of Songs. Solomon was the richest man of his time, but he ended up saying: "Vanity of vanities! All things are vanity," (Eccl. 1:1). Nothing had any value in his eyes save the things money was unable to buy. These are the things of the spirit as well as all the great consolations it is pleasing to God to instill into us. It is God's will we should dispose ourselves for the graces he is only too willing to bestow upon us.

God loves us too much to be satisfied with creating us for this life alone. We are told by St. John that God so loved the world that he gave his only-begotten Son. We should take heart at these words. Not a day should pass in which we should fail to be conscious of our eternal destiny, and the unspeakable joys we shall experience on our departure from this life. Let us anchor the substance of our being on what is immune to change and decay.

Let him kiss me with the kisses of his mouth

We will now turn to the consideration of particular lines in the Song in order to meditate on their analogical meaning.

To begin with the first line: "Let him kiss me with the kisses of his mouth," these words can be applied in prayer to our desire that by means of grace we may become what Christ is by nature.

"The kisses of the mouth," signify the perfect conjunction of God and the soul, a union to be fulfilled only after this life is over.

Such spiritual meanings for "kisses" and then later for such expressions as "your eyes are doves," or "your hair is like a flock of goats," "your rounded thighs like jewels," and "your navel like a rounded bowl," agree with the mystical and allegorical interpretation of the Jews of old prior to the Christian era. All efforts at portraying this divine Canticle as a mere love poem, celebrating purely human affections, have failed miserably to satisfy the soul's craving for something higher than itself with God-like qualities. May it not have been the Song of Songs Our Lord had in view when he said to those around him not to give to dogs what is holy and not to throw pearls before swine (Mt. 7:6)?

"Let him kiss me with the kisses of his mouth," the devout soul says to our divine Lord. In these words she expresses her desire to enter into the state of glory, there to partake of its beatific bliss. In the higher stages of the interior life, we need what the holy angels already possess. It is this necessity the Song of Songs supplies. It does so in divine abundance, and this because of its being celestial in form and quality.

As long as we live, we cannot have the goods of heaven and those of earth also. In asking for the kisses of the mouth, the loving soul says that she wants only that which is of a nature to last forever.

Many there are who have been called by God to sublime states of union with him. The question we must ask ourselves is this: shall we accept so wonderful a grace, or shall we back out for fear of what others may think of us? Shall we settle for some lesser good? The tragedy is that God, being what he is, leaves us free to reject his high gifts and in many cases even to spurn them altogether.

It is not thus with the saints. How many there are who have already received the grace to lay down their lives out of love for the higher teachings of the Christian religion. How many there always will be who will continue to render themselves worthy of so high a calling.

It takes great courage, the masters of the spiritual life tell us, to respond wholeheartedly to the call from God to live lives pleasing to him. This is one of the reasons why so few in every age responded to such a call. With this in mind, let those of us who know better, pray for the grace to avoid making the mistake of setting our sights too low. An eternity of happiness is at stake in the matter of becoming saints.

It is to enable us to become saints that the Song of Songs was written. "Man is nothing, God is all," the blessed Francis Libermann said as he lay dying. Now if God is all, we must measure the rest from the point of view of eternity. God will not fail to provide us with the help we need to accomplish such a purpose. We should not be afraid to ask great things of God, since it is in this way we honor him and pay tribute to his munificence as one who can do great things.

In heaven, we will find in God all we now seek outside of him. The incidental qualities now common to our mortal nature will not be there, but that only in our make-up which resembles the divine nature. It is for these heaven-like qualities the saints asked when they said to Our Lord: "Let him kiss me with the kisses of his mouth, for thy love is better than wine." "Wine" is a symbol for all the good things in this life, when contrasted with those infinitely more wonderful laid up for us in heaven. In asking for the kisses of the mouth, the saints made known to God the love in their hearts for things divine. For them, all the graces they received from God constituted the kisses of the mouth.

Love alone becomes the measure of all things during the final stages of our earthly journey and it is only reasonable that this should be so. In his Epistle to the Corinthians, does not St. Paul himself extol love above every other Christian virtue, since he there tells us "if I speak with human tongues and angelic as well, and do not have love, I am a noisy gong, a clanging cymbal" (1 Cor. 13:1). More and more as we go on living, we realize that love alone matters. For, being what he is, the all-wise and omnipotent one, what is there we his creatures can add to the infinite perfections with which the Godhead is endowed? All we can give him is our love.

And so we sing, "Let him kiss me with the kisses of his mouth."

Your name spoken is a spreading perfume

The "spreading perfume" can be seen as the grace and favors given by God to sanctify the soul. These have been given to us by means of Christ's coming into the world and suffusing it with himself. "We are the aroma of Christ," St. Paul says in reference to himself and those with whom he was intimately united (2 Cor. 2:15).

There is a mystical sense of smell with which the saints inhale into themselves the divine odor of him who is God-made-man. The Hebrew for "smell" is "scent" and "odor." There exists a heavenly unction by means of which Our Lord makes himself present and felt mystically in the substance of the soul. It is of this type of experience the symbolism of the Song speaks.

It is a truism to say that the saints not only know of God but that they also feel him present in their inmost selves. It is this experience of the divine Good Jesus which constitutes the "spreading perfume." In saying to him she loves so much "your name spoken is a spreading perfume," the bride-soul wishes to make known how thoroughly penetrated with the sense of the divine she has become. Suffused with the divine, she is no longer what she has been prior to this experience. By means of this grace, God enables the soul to become what he himself is, though in a limited sense.

It is Christ himself who has revealed himself to the soul, and realizing this to be the case, in her ecstasy, she cries out and says, "your name spoken is a spreading perfume," indicating in these words that something delightful has entered into her.

Tell me, you whom my heart loves, where you pasture your flock, where you give them rest at midday, Lest I be found wandering after the flocks of your companions

The soul which has given itself over completely to the kind of love that shall never end, wants to know Christ better than she does. Knowing the beauty of his being in a more intimate way, she will be safeguarded by means of this experiential knowledge (rest at midday) from setting her affections upon anything which is less than divine (the flocks of your companions).

It is the divine goodness of Jesus which the

soul craves, and so until this goodness is perfectly possessed, she cannot be completely at peace. The soul that loves Christ in the way and manner that she should love him, has nothing to fear from the lesser loves creatures are. Such a person, while still in the body, becomes so completely engulfed and absorbed in the supernatural, that nothing on earth has the power to hinder her loving the good which lasts forever— our divine Lord.

The soul upon which Christ has set the seal of his affection, cannot be satisfied with anything less than himself. It is in the realization of this truth that her earthly happiness lies; that is, in the fact that she has Christ himself for her divine lover, and not any other human being, be that human being wise and beautiful as he/she may be.

Try as she may, such a soul cannot find a substitute for the kind of love Our Lord is, which same love he is more than willing to share with her. She has, by means of grace, been taken into partnership with him who is heaven-sent. How can Christ have any kind of competition? We have small hearts, and so there is only room enough in them for him by whom these hearts of ours have been fashioned. That is not to deny that we can love others *in* Christ as in marriage, friendship, and neighbor-love, but only to assert that the center of our hearts are made for God and no creature can fill that space within us.

As a result of the love of Christ for us, we have

become "partakers in the divine nature," as St. Paul tells us. While there is something deeply human in ourselves, which will always remain so, there is also at the same time something in our inner being which relates us to the angels, and to God himself. Has he not created us in his own image and likeness, namely, in his divine Son?

This image of God, Adam partially lost through sin. But we have something greater. We have Jesus in ourselves, and he will remain there until his expulsion by mortal sin. It is consoling to know that this is so, since it is in our power to have him there in our inner being if we so will. And, who is there who does not will the presence within of the ineffable good Our Lord is? "Thy law is in my intestines," the Psalmist says to God. By the term "law" he makes reference to the law of love, which is Christ.

We have been put on earth to love the kind of love that cannot have an end. This love is Christ. Christ is to us both heaven itself as well as the way thereto, and so we sing with Solomon: "Tell me, you whom my heart loves, where you pasture your flock, where you give them rest at midday, Lest I be found wandering after the flocks of your companions."

> *Ah, you are beautiful, my beloved,*
> *Ah, you are beautiful*

We meditate on the goodness of God, the

justice of God, as well as other attributes, so why should we not also cherish in our hearts the *beauty* of his being? The ancient Greeks spoke of God as the Good, the True, and the Beautiful, and we as Christians can follow in their footsteps in that respect.

"Ah, you are beautiful, my beloved." What sweet words these are for us to address to Christ. Many love beautiful things, but him by whom these beautiful things have been made they do not love. With the saints, though, this is not the case. Instead of resting with the beautiful things God has made, they turn to him who is their blessed author and creator. It is to him they say: "Ah, you are beautiful."

There is a passage in Scripture which speaks of the saints as "studying beautifulness" (Sir. 44:6 Douay version). The prophets of old speak of this beauty of his in many of the oracles they uttered. We are all familiar with Psalm 45 where the Lord is spoken of as being "fairer in beauty...above the sons of men." It is with this in mind we must read the words of the Song of Songs in which speaking of Christ, the bride-soul says, "ah, you are beautiful, my beloved," for beauty sanctifies. It does so because its immortal quality is found in the flesh of Christ.

We love Christ because he is beautiful to contemplate, and this contemplation in turn beautifies us. There is a mutual interchange of praises and it is for this reason we find ourselves so taken up into heaven by the sweet and sublime words of these lines of the Song.

To the Jews of old, beauty of any kind could not exist without that goodness which can come from God alone. "How good thou art," the Semite said to God, and by this he meant to point to God's beauty as well. It is in vain we shall seek for true beauty apart from that goodness which comes to us from the celestial regions.

Christ speaks to us through the nature he has assumed. It is only by means of the Incarnation that we can have a true experience of what God is like. Christ looks at us through his sensible flesh so that we may behold God without harm to our mortal nature. We cannot now see the divine essence, and so it has to be covered by the veil of mortal things. Created things have been made that through them the divine may be perceived, as by so many glances and gleams shining through everything we are, both body and soul. Body and soul, we are a kind of harp for the divine to play on.

The Lord of the universe has stationed himself behind everything we are, so that he may in that way hold intimate communication with our unworthy selves. How entranced we should become at the thought that behind every just person the redeemer of the world has, so to speak, placed himself, so that we may in that way perceive something of his ineffable being!

The Bible is a closed book for those who do not pray for the grace to understand what it has to say. This is especially true in that part of the Scriptures where love alone is so sublimely and so sweetly depicted. Christ is love made flesh. The redeemer of the world is here portrayed in so ardent a manner that those who read its words become enkindled with the fire from heaven— fire nothing on earth is able to extinguish. "I am come to cast fire upon the earth," Our Lord says to us. The "fire" here referred to is that same mystical flame which Moses saw when he beheld the burning bush.

"Ah, you are beautiful, my beloved, ah, you are beautiful." Throughout our entire life in heaven, we shall never cease repeating these words in reference to our divine Lord. There are those who try to get to God without Christ, who is the Way. Hence they never attain the goal for which they have been created; Christ himself is this goal.

To really know the truths of Christianity by personal experience, we have to have the grace to become enraptured by these truths so that, by contemplation of them, we may enter into an ecstasy. It is not the mere theoretical belief in these truths that will enable us to taste the joys of the life to come, but a sort of seizure of them in the depths of our being. It is in the soul's substance that the words are felt which we embrace in an external manner.

There is something within ourselves that enables us to feel what the beauty of Christ is like. When this is brought into play, we cry out in the words of the Song and give utterance to what those words hint at and signify, something infinitely beyond themselves. It is to our divine Lord that these words have reference, as well as to those holy souls who love the beauty of his being with that special love all the saints received from their Father in heaven.

With the saints, this extraordinary love for the beauty of the God-Man begins on earth. The Song of Songs takes us back to that primal happiness enjoyed by our first parents in the Garden of Eden. As we read this Song, the words of the Psalmist come to our minds in which he says, "Woe is me that I sojourn in Mesech, that I dwell amid the tents of Kedar!" These words give expression to our regret at still finding ourselves in the present life, instead of the eternity the Song makes us wish for so intensely.

No true believer in the God-Man and lover of his beauty, permits him/herself to become sad and depressed, since sadness proves that this belief in God is not the genuine thing it is meant to be. Referring to those who have given themselves over to the pursuit of what passes away with time, the prophet Job asks: "Can such people delight themselves in the Almighty?" Can such have him for the exclusive object of their love?

The obvious answer to this question is that they cannot. They are incapable of loving two different things at once, time and eternity. We look not on the things that are seen, we say with St. Paul, but on the things that are not seen. We of the faith should focus the affections of our hearts and minds on what the bodily eye is unable to behold—unperceivable realities and unseen values which Our Lord brought with him upon his entry into the glory of his heavenly Kingdom.

From the moment of our entry into this life until our departure from it, we are filled with evils of every kind. It is for this reason God finds it difficult to be too hard on us. It is for this reason, too, that his mercy determines the attitude he has towards us. God knows that we are sinners and that, as such, we are made to suffer the consequences of our wrong doings. In the Song of Songs, the divine love of Christ solves all our earthly problems, they are solved by means of the love he himself gives us.

The devout soul comes to this Song after its clash with earth's values, this Song holding up to it those of heaven. "I have fought the good fight," St. Paul says as he finds himself nearing the end of his earthly days. By fighting the "good fight," he means to indicate that there can be no compromise with the standards of time and those that are set forth in the Gospel writings. Time allures us with its momentary pleasures; but those of eternity exert upon us a more powerful and lasting influence. We have to choose, and we do so by the love for Christ depicted in the Song of Songs.

"Bring me, O king, to your chambers," the soul cries out to Christ, "and we will run after thee." The word for "bring" in Hebrew means draw. The soul asks to be drawn into the chambers of God because it finds nothing worth pursuing in this life. Only the beauty of Christ depicted in this Song is without any restrictions and qualifications, God being beauty itself in its uncreated state.

How unhappy they must be who cannot love beauty made flesh in the Person of Christ! Of what ecstatic bliss all such are deprived by the lack of this love! How we must thank God to be able to love the beauty of his divine Son! "You are beautiful, my beloved," we will say to Christ and we shall continue doing so for all eternity, and it will be in the repetition of these words that our beatitude will consist.

Our couch, too, is verdant

The Hebrew for "couch" is divan, and by "verdant" luxuriousness is indicated. In a mystical way, these words point to the fact that unless we make Christ the main source of our earthly delight, we can neither know nor love him. It was for this reason we find God saying to us: "This is my beloved Son in whom I am well pleased" (Mt. 17:5), corroborating the words of the Song of Songs in which we are told how beautiful Our Lord is.

Without delight in the Lord we do not know what Christianity is, let alone the whole body of the Church's truths such as the Holy Trinity, the Incarnation. In the Song of Songs our divine Lord has laid upon us the burden of his love. We cannot love him unless we find him beautiful to contemplate and muse upon with our whole hearts and with our whole minds. Hence the image of verdant luxuriousness.

Without love and delight, the person of Our Lord becomes estranged from us and the means of union with him is taken away. "Take delight in the Lord," the Psalmist says to us, "and he will grant you your heart's requests" (Ps. 37:4). To obtain all we wish for in this life, we have to find our whole delight in him. This will make us happy.

It is the will of our Father in heaven that Christ should be the soul's rest. When we read words such as "you are beautiful, my beloved, yes, you are lovely... our couch, too, is verdant," that is, refreshing and luxuriating, we should apply these words to that inner peace of soul, the divine tranquility which they enjoy who do all in their power to make Christ the object of their earthly delight.

Apart from delight in God, these men and women cannot live the kind of life intended by him. God has from all eternity loved us in his divine Son. It is for this reason he wishes we should find in him the kind of delight with which no other delight can be compared. Then we shall cry out "our couch, too, is verdant."

I delight to rest in his shadow,
and his fruit is sweet to my mouth

We will search in vain throughout the Scriptures for a greater law than the law of love for Christ. It is by this holy means Almighty God wills that we should regulate our earthly lives. It is by the law of love of Christ that we shall attain to what God wishes on our behalf.

God is love, and so, to have a personal experience of what he is like, we have to make use of the means he provides. St. Augustine tells us that those who are proud resent God's becoming man, and that their wish is for him to remain inaccessible to us. The Incarnation brings God close to us. This is the reason for the complaint of the proud against the teachings of Christianity. They hold themselves aloof from these teachings at all costs. Those who suffer from spiritual and intellectual pride are shocked to hear Our Lord call himself our brother, our inmost friend, our fellow-kinsman. But in answer to such sinful aloofness on the part of those who lack humility and remain away from the Church, we find these words: "I delight to rest in his shadow, and his fruit is sweet to my mouth."

He brings me into his banquet hall
and his emblem over me is love

Love is the standard of eternity and it is by means of it that everything is there regarded. Love makes saints and the lack of it those who are opposed to them.

There are certain souls that cannot come to God unless he places before them certain allurements, those in the Song of Songs are the most overpowering. No threats of any kind can affect such people but only charms and raptures of the sweetest kind. In this respect, the Song of Songs is the sweetmeat of the soul, since in it she finds that which fills her with heavenly and paradisiacal delight. There is no place in the banquet hall of heaven for anything but love. Whatever is not love is left behind, interred in the grave with our mortal frame. In the life to come we shall see God, and God, we are told, is love.

"He brings me into his banquet hall and his emblem over me is love." Love exalts us in Christ Jesus and love only. No other virtue can replace love, since it is by means of love that we go to heaven. Love for Our Lord is the "flaming chariot" by which Elijah went up to heaven (2 Kgs. 2:11).

"He brings me into the banquet hall and his emblem over me is love." In Hebrew, "banquet hall" means house of wine. The mystical gifts of the saints are in this Song compared to a wine cellar, filling the souls thus favored with all manner of exquisite delights. Love leads us to God and the absence of it takes us away from him, there being no substitute for this divine and heaven-sent gift.

By means of the Incarnation, God has enriched our human nature with himself. Try as we may, we cannot return to the sense of values of this world prior to the coming of Christ into it. In the rejection of Christ the Saviour by some of the Jews of old, the love he brought with him from his Father in heaven was spurned. But after Christ's coming into the world we cannot live without the kind of love he himself is.

"Oh that thou wert my brother," we say to our divine Lord, "then I should find thee...and I would kiss thee." There is no need to point out that this "kiss" of which the Song speaks is the mystical embrace of the divine bridegroom, Jesus, of which all the saints have spoken in such obscure and hidden terms. The saints covered their feeling for Christ in figurative language. They did so lest those who knew him not would be baffled and scandalized by their words. On earth we need enigmatic terminology. In the next life, we shall no longer be afraid to say openly to Christ all we feel concerning himself and his beauty.

Yes, his banner over me is love, for it is by means of love that Our Lord rules the world and prepares for those who love him what "eye has not seen, nor ear heard, nor what it has so much as dawned upon man to conceive."

God's love is shed abroad in the hearts of the saints so that they may by its means light up the world and enkindle it with what will last forever. God is love and it is because of this that we are believing and hopeful human beings looking forward to the banquet hall, having over us the emblem of love.

Strengthen me with raisin cakes, refresh me with apples, for I am faint with love

Certainly these words mean more than they imply in their ordinary usage. Spiritually and mystically they signify the well-being of the soul both in this life and the next.

We cannot know for certain now what those pleasures (raisin cakes and apples) were which our first parents enjoyed before they sinned.

However, no matter what they were, we know for certain that God was the origin of them. Prior to the sin of disobedience, Adam and Eve were in possession of an uninterrupted communion with God, now lost to us.

Before sin was committed, there was no need for suffering in order to know God. Now, however, there is such a need. We cannot now enter into the kingdom of heaven except through the "many tribulations" of which St. Paul speaks. This makes us realize how grievous a thing sin is, for by its means we have been deprived of the enjoyment that comes from uninterrupted communion with the divine.

In the life to come, we will regain the fullness of the good things of God Adam had before he sinned. In the meantime, our love for Christ acts as a kind of medicine to the soul. It is to this type of healing of the wounds of sin that these words refer: "Strengthen me with raisin cakes, refresh me with apples, for I am faint with love."

> *Hark! my lover—here he comes,*
> *springing across the mountains,*
> *leaping across the hills*

Christ comes to us all the time. He does so by means of his own inspirations, through the beautiful thoughts instilled into our hearts by the agency of the holy angels, in Scripture, the sacraments, our encounters with others throughout the day.

We are told by St. Augustine that we should hear the voice of Christ in all the Psalms. But what is this voice of Christ which all the saints heard speaking to them from the pages of Holy Writ? Certainly it is not the kind of sound made audible in the ear of the flesh. The voice speaks to us, instead, substantially in the depths of the soul.

All throughout the Old Testament writings, God finds fault with the Jewish people for their failure to trust in his divine Son and to look to him for security and safety. This lack of faith in the redeemer of the world, who was coming, is especially brought out in the Book of Psalms, for we read there: "because they believed not in God, and trusted not in his salvation" (Ps. 78:22). Now St. Jerome pointed out that "salvation" in Hebrew *is a noun*, and it has reference to Christ! Throughout the Sacred Scriptures, we are bidden to take refuge in Christ, so that we may make him alone the source of our safety and security.

Someone said that "it is hard to find a man competent to scale the heights of the Song of Songs, even though he has traversed all the songs in the Scriptures." It is for this reason the Canticle of Canticles has been named the Song of Songs, like the holy of holies—it is above everything else that has ever been written. Nothing else in all literature is able to raise up the human spirit to such heights. Why are there so few who have the grace to be able to penetrate into the sweet and sublime mystery this Song mirrors forth? The answer to this lies in the sad fact that there are few who, by the way they live, dispose themselves for the heavenly secrets of divine love disclosed in it. All the prophets have spoken of the Messiah who is one day to come in the flesh. But none of them have described the beauty of his being in a way so sweet as did the Jewish king Solomon. All the saints, especially all the great contemplative ones, have made this Song their very own.

"Behold, here he comes." Some day this coming of his will be final. When this shall take place we will be blessed forever. As long as we live, we are looking forward to the day when we shall attain our heavenly state in the life to come.

Our Lord comes to us in an infinite number of ways, but in order to be able to recognize these comings of his, we have to be saints. "Come, Lord Jesus," we will all say the moment we are about to depart from this life to become what he himself is.

"Springing across the mountains, leaping across the hills." Prior to the Incarnation, Our Lord came to us in the person of the saints who lived before that time. It was they who constituted the "mountains" spoken of in the Song of Songs, on account of the sublimity of their views about God and their longing to be with him in perfect union. With this truth before us, we should continually say: "Hark! my lover—here he comes, springing across the mountains, leaping across the hills."

My lover...stands behind our walls,
gazing through the windows,
peering through the lattices

The "wall" may be interpreted as our human nature, our mortality, acting as a kind of wall separating us from the immortal joys of the life to come. The "wall" can be thought of as the flesh in its present unglorified state which constitutes an impediment to complete and perfect union with the Ineffable.

The "lattices" can be seen as designating the senses of the body through which the goodness of Jesus is filtered, or through which he glimpses us and we him. "Lattices" could also be the human body of Christ in which God's divinity is veiled, for otherwise we could not see him and live. God became man that the divine should become part of our lives, mingled with our own selves. Yet there is still the veil. For as long as we live we are kept from the full sight of the divine beauty of him we love so much. He is "standing behind our walls, gazing through the windows, peering through the lattices."

My lover speaks: He says to me,
'arise, my beloved, my beautiful one,
and come! For see, the winter is past,
the rains are over and gone.
The flowers appear on the earth; and
the song of the dove is heard in our land'

"Arise, my beloved, my beautiful one, and come!" In these words Christ beckons us to himself. Our Lord asks us to draw near to him as they do who are already in heaven.

More and more as we meditate on the truths of our faith, we realize that it is heaven that counts for our happiness and not this poor earth with all the sorrows to be met upon it. "Prepare to meet your God, O Israel" (Am. 4:12).

In everything that exists Christ asks us to come to him. The goodness and beauty in things are so many voices calling to us to come to him through whom they have been created.

It is the Risen Christ who speaks to us here, and not the one laid in the tomb Good Friday. The Song of Songs speaks to us of our Risen Lord, and this is why it is so consoling to read and meditate upon. We are lonely in this life because in it he whom we love so much is not fully possessed. Yet we hear the voice of the Lord calling to us "arise, my beloved, my beautiful one, and come," inviting us to one day share in his eternal felicity.

"The winter is past...the song of the dove is heard in our land...." The Douay version of the Song has here "the time of singing has come," calling to mind the line from the Psalms "sing to the Lord a new song."

This new spring-song of the "dove" may be viewed as the song of faith in the Resurrection chanted by Christian believers. We sing this song because "the winter" of death has been conquered by Christ for us. The "winter" of this present life will soon be over and gone. Easter day will be ours forever.

We rejoice in the Resurrection as we do in no other Christian reality, for by its holy means all our earthly woes are brought to an end. "What misery is there," St. Jerome asks, "for which belief in the Resurrection does not console?"

"The flowers appear on the earth...." The flowers are a figure of the truths of our salvation announced in the four Gospels. They may also be seen as the flowers of sanctity won by Christ's victory over death.

"The song of the dove is heard in our land," in that our hearts are overjoyed at the good news of the Resurrection. In the Vulgate, "time of pruning" also means "time of singing," and so this phrase is also one of jubilation.

My dove, hiding in the clefts of the rock

What a lot of suffering there is in the world today. Much of it is due to lack of faith in the promises of Christ. What a great deal of misery people would rid themselves of if they asked for the grace to root themselves in the Heart of Christ. This rooting ourselves in the Heart of Christ constitutes the "clefts of the rock" mentioned in the Song of Songs.

"Come to me all you who labor and are wearied and I will give you rest," Our Lord says to us. The "rest" here promised is none other than that refreshment of soul Adam and Eve experienced before they sinned. How unwise people are not to love Christ, since it is by means of this love for him that they would find the solution to all that troubles them so much. Let us hide in the "cleft" of his heart.

Christ came to take our troubles away from us, and he does this by means of our faith in him. Without this surrender on our part, he can do nothing, for unbelief ties his hands. With faith we live, not just vegetate; living in faith already in God's high heaven which may be called the "clefts of the rock."

With this in mind, is it any wonder the saints valued faith so much and did all in their power to increase it in themselves? *Faith* here includes trust in the infinite wisdom, mercy, power, and love of the God-Man—our "rock."

Let me see you, let me hear your voice,
for your voice is sweet, and you are lovely

We have been made for the divine vision, and
so until it is bestowed upon us, we cannot be
completely at rest in this life. God came to us in
the person of his divine Son, since it is only in that
way the Creator of the universe could be made
apprehensible to us.

"Let me see your face," the soul says to Christ.
The word "face" refers here to the whole mystical reality of Christ's presence.

"Let me hear your voice." The voice of Christ
has an intoxicating effect upon those who listen
to it with love.

We live in hope of seeing that face and hearing
that voice. What, after all, is the use of living
unless we make Christ the exclusive object of our
hope? What's the use of going through all the
pain and misery unless we have in ourselves the
hope from heaven Our Lord came to bring? What
is the use of putting up with everything unless
we get the grace to be able to believe in all he
came on earth to teach and reveal to us?

Without Christ and the love for him deeply
rooted in our inner being, what is there for a
reasonable human being worth getting excited
about? Is not everything a sham and a mockery
without Christ? And does it not end up in the

utter nothingness of which the prophets have spoken? Without faith in Christ it were better we had never been born, since apart from his truth all is deceit and lies.

When we love Christ and believe in all he came on earth to communicate to us, we find there is a craving in ourselves to become what he himself is. We want to identify ourselves with his own beautiful and blessed being—his "face" and his "voice." The desired identity is not a proud usurping of the attributes of the Godhead, but rather a humble creaturely longing to become by means of love what the Lover himself is. The Christian who loves Christ does not want to wait until she sees him in heaven. She craves a taste of his sweetness right here on this earth. And she has been encouraged to do so by the Psalmist—"taste and see that the Lord is sweet." Since this tasting of the divine good that Jesus is takes place in a mystical manner, it cannot be spoken of in a clear and precise way. Instead we speak in allegory as in the Song.

In the words of St. John we cry out, "Come quickly, Lord Jesus." "Show me thy glory," Moses was not afraid to say to the all-powerful, all-merciful, and all-loving God. God wants us to have daring wishes and daring hopes. We should not be afraid to ask great things from God, the saints tell us, since it is in this way we honor him most.

To become saints, we must set no limit to our

desires as far as Christ is concerned. It is this extreme, intense, unrestricted ardor which renders us pleasing to him. And so, with this in mind, how shall we be afraid to say in time and in eternity: "Let me see you, let me hear your voice, for your voice is sweet, and you are lovely."

My lover belongs to me, and I to him

"My lover belongs to me and I to him." The bride-soul here means that as the result of her love she has been transformed into its object, who is none other than Christ the Lord.

In the mystical state, a union occurs which renders the soul and God as if they were one sole reality. Because of this experience there have been false mystics who have confounded the distinction there remains between the Creator and the creatures made by him. What we believe is that regardless of the unity between the soul and God in prayer, there remains a difference in substance. God is what he is, and the soul is what she is. There is, however, a oneness by means of love, and it is to this unity the Song refers when the words are used "my lover belongs to me and I to him."

"Thou art I, and I am thou," Our Lord said to Blessed Angela of Foligno, indicating that even in this life one may experience the union we all will enjoy in the life to come. In Hebrew the expression, "My lover is mine and I am his," can be translated to mean that when love is "strong as death," as the Song of Songs proclaims, the two, God and the soul, become by grace one sole reality. They become mystically blended together, as indeed they will be after this life is over. Our happiness on earth consists in the moral certainty that by means of grace we become one with him, in a love which consumes in us everything which is not God. We live for Christ and so, out of his great love for us, he in a way lives for us!

"My lover belongs to me and I to him." We must continually keep on saying these words to ourselves so that we may rise to the heights of love desired for us by an infinitely loving Lord. It is not God's fault that men are unhappy, but their own, since they fail to dwell on him who is happiness itself, letting hope neutralize the sorrow and pain in their hearts. Dwelling on Christ we become partakers of his own divine joys which are infinite in extent. "Come unto me all you who labor and are heavy laden and I will give you rest."

"Myself am hell," John Milton makes Satan say. The good angel could have said "myself am heaven." We must in the present life look for heaven in our own souls. We will succeed in finding it nowhere else. Foolish human beings! We are possessed of the facility of avoiding loving what can alone make us happy. In the life to come, the problems we have will no longer exist. There we will not be free to love that which is not divine. The full and clear vision of God will draw our hearts into unity with him.

"My lover belongs to me and I to him." These words signify the highest state of the human spirit attainable in this life—the spiritual marriage. Doctors of mystical theology claim that after this there is nothing but the glory of the beatific vision in heaven. We cannot enter heaven while we live, but we may, if God so wills, stand in the vestibule or antechamber, where mystics are transformed in Christ.

"My lover belongs to me, and I to him." This is a very consoling truth. We should never fail to cherish in our hearts the belief that an intimacy exists between God and our own selves, which intimacy nothing on earth is able to dissolve or to destroy. We must think of God and of ourselves, not as alone, but as one by means of grace. Men and women are lonely in this life. They are sad and depressed, letting gloom insinuate itself in their hearts, because they do not enter into union with Christ. Christ loves us. We must think of this every moment of the day. Otherwise we cannot be at peace with ourselves or with any other human being. God loves us. If he did not, we would not be. As long as we live, Christ must constitute the food of our souls. Without this food, the soul dies.

And so being drawn into union with our God, we sing, "My lover belongs to me and I to him."

On my bed at night, I sought him
whom my heart loves.
I sought him, but I did not find him.
I will rise then and go about the city,
in the streets and crossings
I will seek him whom my heart loves.
I sought him but I did not find him

God created the universe so that by means of everything in it we might be able to seek him "whom our heart loves." Everything that God has made is for the purpose of reflecting in itself the divine, chief among these being the soul of man. God, it has been said, created the world to be a kind of book to us, in which his handwriting, in the form of its many wonders, can be detected. After this life is over, we will clearly see how everything we came in contact with in this world was meant to lead us to him who always is, the "wonderful one" mentioned in the book of Isaiah.

With this truth vividly before us, we say to Our Lord the words of the Song, which tell us that the purpose of our life in this world is always to "rise" and seek him whom our heart loves.

The soul is on a constant lookout in this life for what it will one day enjoy to the full in the world to come. Our Lady told St. Bernadette that she would not make her happy in the present life, but in the one to come. "I sought him but I did not find him," we say in reference to what will one day be a source of unending happiness to us and what has been made known to the human race by the Incarnation of Christ.

"By night on my bed I sought him whom my soul loves: I sought him, but found him not." They who crave for something divine can find that craving satisfied in Christ alone, since he is the one who has placed that craving for himself in their hearts. And so, unless such people know this to be the case, they will spend all their lives in pursuit of what cannot be had in anything else that God has made.

"I will rise then and go about the city...." By the term "rise" we are urged to bestir ourselves to love him by whom and for whom and through whom all things are what they are, ourselves included. It is God's will that we should love everything we are, both body and soul, in his divine Son, for whose sake we have been created.

The purpose of our life in this world is to become other Christs. We must always be on the lookout for Christ. The Song of Songs tells us this, but it does so in a figurative way and not in

the open and clear way of the New Testament.
Christ is the heaven for which we have been
brought into being and into which we shall enter
upon our departure from this life. And so we
sing: "On my bed at night I sought him whom my
heart loves. I sought him but I did not find him. I
will rise then and go about the city, in the streets
and crossings I will seek him whom my heart
loves. I sought him but I did not find him."

The watchmen came upon me
as they made their rounds of the city:
Have you seen him whom my heart loves?

These "watchmen" can be symbolic of the holy
angels by means of whom God holds converse
with us in a supernatural way. They are his
messengers to us and ours to him.

There is a beautiful reference to these holy
spirits in the book of Exodus. God there says to
every one of us: "See, I am sending an angel
before you to the place I have prepared. Be atten-
tive to him and heed his voice" (Ex. 23:20). It has
been an unbroken tradition, both before and
after Christianity, that God sends these holy
spirits to guard us on the way to himself, so it is
for this reason we must relate to them lovingly.
Oftentimes in our relationship with him, God
does not deal with us directly, but through the
intermediary of the blessed spirits. It is for this

reason that the soul who loves God says the above quoted words of the Song of Songs. We know that the angels help us to find our way to the sublime and exalted things of the most high God.

St. John Chrysostom has said that upon our departure from the body, the soul will be conducted by an angel to her proper place in the life to come, and without this aid the soul could never find her way there. In reference to the holy angels, another saint said these words: "Angels are all light." By the word "light" he did not mean something we can see with the eyes of the body, but rather what we "see" in a spiritual manner in the part of us which resembles the light of glory in the life to come.

"Have you seen him whom my soul loves," the bride here asks the spirits created for the purpose of lifting up our hearts to the contemplation of things divine. We cannot find our way to eternal happiness without the aid of those who are already in full possession of this joy.

We are all familiar with the words of the Ninety-first Psalm "though a thousand fall at your side, ten thousand at your right, near you it shall not come, for to his angels he has given command about you, that they guard you in all your ways" (Ps. 91:7). When it comes to the sanctification of our lives God has left nothing to chance. Every detail of our relationship with him has been worked out from all eternity.

Until this takes place, we sometimes count the hours that pass, wishing to find ourselves closer to the place of our heart's desire.

God is infinitely good. It is for this reason he makes us undergo trials as a means to get to know what the joys of God are like. Sorrow exists to enable us to get to know what heaven is like, by contrast. We cannot love in a Christian way unless we live the kind of life Our Lord himself went through while he was among men. "What little sense you have," Our Lord is always telling us. "What little sense you have! How slow you are to believe all that the prophets announced! Did not the Messiah have to undergo all this so as to enter into his glory?" (Lk. 24:23).

We cannot enter into heaven unless we go through the tribulations of this life, and it was to point this out that after Adam and Eve had sinned, God placed a cherubim (watchman) at the east of Eden with a "fiery revolving sword" symbolizing the suffering and pain we have to experience if we are to receive a taste of those joys our first parents had before they sinned. All this shows that heaven can be had—but at the price of suffering.

And so we call upon the angels to show us the face of God hidden in our sufferings: "the watchmen came upon me as they made their rounds of the city: have you seen him whom my heart loves?"

Let my lover come to his garden
to eat its choice fruits

More than an ordinary love for Christ is necessary if we are to get a taste on earth of what the joys of heaven are like. We must make up our minds to love Christ with the same passionate intensity of the bride-soul of the Song of Songs.

We have to pray for the Holy Spirit to enter into the garden of our soul so as to infuse this kind of love into us. "Let my lover come to his garden to eat its choice fruits." These fruits are the gifts of the Holy Spirit by means of which we are enabled to love Our Lord in the way they do who are no longer in this life.

We must love him with everything we are—both body and soul. If we do this, we too shall have that rest in heaven the blessed enjoy. Our Lord wishes we should repose in him. That is why he said: "Come to me, all you who are weary and find life burdensome, and I will refresh you" (Mt. 11:28). Our Lord is here referring to that Sabbath rest we shall one day have in the life to come, the beginning of which consists in the contemplation of the beauty of his being of which the Song of Songs speaks in so sublime a manner.

We can also interpret the garden image as meaning that Christ is the garden of the soul, and the soul in its turn the garden of Christ. In the Old Testament writings, the Creator of the universe is spoken of as walking in the Garden of Eden. The souls of believers are a place of delight for the Lord. And when we love the Lord we love as well the souls of those who have by means of grace been enshrined in him. And so we sing, "let my lover come to his garden, and eat its choice fruits."

I was sleeping, but my heart kept vigil

The Hebrew word for "sleep" means to be "changed." It can conveniently be applied to the task of converting ourselves into him who is our all. Another signification of the term "sleep" is the idea of transferring something into another place. We must transfer ourselves into the unchanging One, namely, Christ the Lord. It is into him we must become totally assimilated insofar as this is possible under the conditions of this life. Our total immersion in the God-Man will take place at the moment of death and not until then. In the meantime, we are told in this beautiful Canticle, to do what is in our power to become like unto him—the beloved, the beautiful one, with whose being our own will one blessed day be blended.

The "sleep" here referred to has nothing to do with bodily slumber when our eyes are closed in the rest we take at night. Sleep here points to that quietude of the soul when all its faculties are stilled during the time given over to the contemplation of divine truths. At such times nothing is understood in an ordinary way.

The sleep here spoken of concerns the transformation of the soul in Christ, so that by means of God's special grace, it no longer thinks and feels apart from God. In such a mystical experience, that which is in heaven is communicated by God in the substance of the soul.

"My heart kept vigil," means that we stirred up in ourselves the love of Christ. In a secondary sense the words "keeping vigil" also mean to rejoice and to be glad. If we love someone or something, we are always stirred up. We are always aroused and awakened by what we love, and this in turn causes us to be conscious of the joy the object of this love brings with it.

We must always be on the alert to stir up in ourselves love for him who alone is worthy of our entire heart's concern and our whole mind's regard. There is nothing incidental when it comes to loving God. We must be sure we meditate on God in such a way that he is properly cherished and appreciated.

"My heart kept vigil." We never tire talking to others about someone we love very much, nor do we weary of extolling whatever attractive qualities we find in such a person. Now, if we do not fail to do this in reference to a human being, why should we hesitate to do so in reference to him

who is the Lord of the universe? This is exactly
what the bride-soul does in the Song of Songs,
for she sings there of him whom she loves very
much and does so in a way which is unique. The
soul that loves God very much can never tire of
giving outward expression of this love for him,
and this no matter how extravagant such expressions may sound to those who have through their
own fault forfeited such love.

And so we sing: "I was sleeping, but my heart
kept vigil."

Open to me, my sister, my love, my dove, my perfect one

"Open to me," Our Lord says to each of us,
open to me, and not only to the infinite number
of good and beautiful things which have been
wrought by my power, mercy, and wisdom. God
became man that man might in that way become
what God himself is, supernatural and divine.

"Open to me," Our Lord is continually saying
to each of us. "Open to me," and to the infinity of
good and beautiful things which we shall one day
enjoy in the life to come. We cannot be satisfied
by the goodness and beauty of any created thing,
and so it is for this reason the Psalmist proclaims,
"I shall be satisfied when thy glory shall appear."

"Open to me, my sister, my beloved, my dove,

my perfect one." A time will come in our lives when there will be no place to go but heaven. All other doors will be shut in a bewildering number of ways. One reason for this is that as we grow older our health declines, our friends die one by one, and we find ourselves put aside by those who are young in years. All this is God's way of saying to us that we should look forward to going to heaven as the sole solution to all these problems. They come about precisely to convince us that this world is not our true homeland but only a kind of makeshift place where we learn how to love what lasts forever.

"Light, more light," the greatest poet Germany ever produced, Goethe, cried out as he lay dying. We, too, need the kind of light Christ is, or we will never find our way to him. We must open our hearts and minds to the influences of heaven. God and his holy angels are constantly beckoning to us in the form of these holy stirrings we call inspirations. God is always calling out to us and saying, open to me, my sister, my beloved one. As we go on living, these words take on additional emphasis by the mere fact that we find no lasting satisfaction in anything this life has to offer. As we go on living, we find that there is no place to go but to him who is everything.

To cheer themselves on their way to heaven, the saints of the Old Testament used to sing songs. We, today, following their example, must also sing. As the Psalmist says, "Sing to the Lord a new song," the one that is Christ. "How shall we sing the song of the Lord in a foreign land?" the Jews of old used to ask. They were making reference to the foreign land of the present life. For this reason, all the time we live, we must entertain ourselves with holy festivals. Thus engaged, our exile in this life will be more bearable. The words of the Song of Songs provide an ideal way to occupy our minds and hearts for they speak of him who will one day constitute our all.

In the words of St. Paul, "we have here no lasting city." Everything that we go through has an end. Nothing is left but that vision of peace which the name Jerusalem signifies and which in turn is symbolic of the beatific state.

"Open to me, my sister, my love," he who loves us so much tells us, from whose existence all other existence proceeds. Open to me, Our Lord says, because I am the One to whom you should direct all the energies of your heart and mind. Open to me, because I alone am capable of satisfying all the desires of your heart. Open to me, because, in the words of Moses, I am he who always is, I am being itself. Open to me because I alone am infinitely beautiful. Open to me, for I am the "desired of all nations," of whom the prophet spoke.

Set me as a seal on your heart,
as a seal on your arm;
For stern as death is love,
relentless as the nether world is devotion;
its flames are a blazing fire

If there is one thing the Song of Songs is trying to convey to us, it is that the highest state of relationship with God is that of love. In that state it is as if we do not even need faith anymore, so present to us is our beloved, so much are we "sealed" to him.

"Its flames are a blazing fire." Love is a divine fire, consuming everything contrary to itself. Through suffering in union with our divine Lord, we become by grace what he himself is in essence and nature. Suffering purifies the soul. Without the purification effected in us by Christian suffering, we would not know by personal experience who and what Christ is.

"Its flames are a blazing fire." There exists a mystical and supernatural kind of fire. This "fire" is the consuming love for Christ. The Song tells us that we should love Christ in a deeply mystical way, so we can know what he is like. Mere belief in him does not provide the soul with the full and perfect knowledge it is meant by God to have.

"Its flames are a blazing fire," could also signify the "flame of Jahweh." Throughout the Old Testament we are told that God is a consuming fire of love, absorbing the soul into himself by means of this love.

St. John of the Cross, taking a hint from this appellation for God, entitled one of his mystical treatises *The Living Flame of Love.* Christ is a living flame of love, consuming the soul not with the ardor of his wrath, but with that of his love. It is love alone that unites us to God. The lack of it causes separation from him. When we have attained to the degree of love for himself God has ordained from all eternity, then God takes us to himself by means of a holy and happy death. What is death, but the complete transformation in the love of Christ?

And so we sing: "Set me as a seal on your heart, as a seal on your arm; for stern as death is love, relentless as the nether world is devotion; its flames are a blazing fire."

Deep waters cannot quench love,
nor floods sweep it away

We cannot live without the love Christ is. Realizing that this is so, we do all we can to transform ourselves into what Our Lord himself is, into the kind of love for which no name can be found.

There is something delightfully incomprehensible in every human being God has made, and it is composed of the God-like love that dwells in that person. God is love, and so to be what he himself is, that love must transform us more and more.

In the higher stages of the spiritual life, God rules us by means of the love he himself is. And thus being dominated by him, we enter into a kind of ecstasy, unquenchable by changing tides.

"Many waters cannot quench love," we are told by the Holy Spirit as he speaks to us through the mouth of Solomon, who knew by personal experience all that love is. Affectionate hearts love Christ, and those who are devoid of this affection know him not, until they obtain it. Until then they fail to have that loving knowledge of him possessed by all the saints. The world is composed of two sets of people: those who come to know by personal experience the love Christ is, and those who, for reasons not clear to us in this life, do not hear of or disdain that love. Let us pray to have that grace-filled love that cannot be quenched by many waters.

Be swift, my lover, like a gazelle
or a young stag on the mountain of spices

Heaven, not earth, is the goal of the believer in Christ, but heaven begun in this life. It is for this reason that the last verse in the Song of Songs deals with the time when we shall, by means of the grace of death, be called home. Yes, Our Lord says to the souls in love with him, "be swift, my lover, like a gazelle or a young stag on the mountain of spices." Mystically, these words denote the entry of the soul into the state of blessedness.

Out of his infinite goodness and love, God keeps us in this world until it becomes absolutely clear to us that what we are looking for cannot be found in it. In the Song of Songs Our Lord is spoken of in a way which renders the beauty of his being irresistible. In it, the soul is beckoned to take flight to the heights of his divinity, since it is there alone that all its God-instilled cravings can be appeased.

"Be swift, my lover," God says to us every single moment of the day and night, indicating in these words that it is his will that we should long for him exclusively.

With every moment that passes, the craving for what is divine is intensified in us, and this, in turn, renders our earthly days less and less bearable. St. Margaret Mary said that she "could think of no greater sacrifice than that of having to live." If we were as holy as she, we would think like her, and so the word "heaven" would be constantly on our lips and never absent from our hearts.

Men and women are time-conscious and time-centered and it is in this their misery lies. If they asked God for the grace to be eternity-minded, many of the problems they have would be automatically solved for them by this eternity-mindedness!

"Be swift, my lover, like a gazelle or a young stag on the mountain of spices." The "mountain" is the height of all the good things Our Lord is, which it is his will to share with us. By thinking his thoughts and living his life, we become divinized. "When shall I go and behold the face of God?" (Ps. 42:3) has been the cry of all the saints. If we are to join their own blessed society we must say the same thing with them.

When the time arrives for us to leave this life, we must flee away to the "mountain of spices," which are the truths of the faith, and take refuge in these truths as a way of salvation and sanctification. All the unimagined wealth of heaven draws close to us as we approach the end of this life's journey. There is joy in the heart as we read this Song and meditate on its sweet words. "Be swift, my lover, like a gazelle or a young stag, on the mountain of spices."

Finale

"I long to depart and be with Christ," wrote St. Paul. It is not so much this life that counts, but the amount of love we accumulate in it for our neighbor and for him who is love itself.

After reading commentaries such as our own, the Song of Songs, begins to enter into us. We begin to truly believe what the words of the Song tell us of sublime joy and delight. A sort of window is opened so that we can see what is waiting for us in the life to come. We begin to understand the saying of Rabbi Akiba that "the whole world is not worth the day when this Song was given to the people of Israel."

The Song of Songs will always be the favorite book of the whole Scripture. May we leave this life with its words deeply rooted in our hearts and minds, since no greater favor than this can be bestowed upon us at such an awesome time.

May we sing once more—

The Song of Songs

Let him kiss me with the kisses of his mouth...
   Your name spoken is a spreading perfume...
Tell me, you whom my heart loves,
   where you pasture your flock,
where you give them rest at midday,
      Lest I be found wandering

after the flocks of your companions...
Ah, you are beautiful, my beloved,
    ah, you are beautiful...
        Our couch, too, is verdant...
I delight to rest in his shadow,
    and his fruit is sweet to my mouth...
He brings me into his banquet hall,
        and his emblem over me is love...
    Strengthen me with raisin cakes,
        refresh me with apples,
    for I am faint with love...
Hark! my lover—here he comes,
    springing across the mountains,
        leaping across the hills...
My lover stands behind our wall,
    gazing through the windows,
        peering through the lattices...
My lover speaks: he says to me, 'arise,
    my beloved, my beautiful one,
        and come! For see
        the winter is past,
        the rains are over and gone.
The flowers appear on the earth;
    and the song of the dove
        is heard in our land'...
My dove, hiding in the clefts of the rock...
Let me see you, let me hear your voice,
    for your voice is sweet,
        and you are lovely...
        My lover belongs to me, and I to him...
On my bed at night, I sought him

whom my heart loves.
I sought him, but I did not find him.
I will rise then and go about the city,
in the streets and crossings
I will seek him whom my heart loves.
I sought him but I did not find him...
The watchmen came upon me as they made
their rounds of the city:
Have you seen him whom my heart loves?...
Let my lover come to his garden
to eat its choice fruits...
I was sleeping, but my heart kept vigil...
Open to me, my sister, my love,
my dove, my perfect one...
Set me as a seal on your heart,
as a seal on your arm;
For stern as death is love,
relentless as the nether world is devotion;
its flames are a blazing fire.
Deep waters cannot quench love,
nor floods sweep it away.
Be swift, my lover,
like a gazelle or a young stag
on the mountain of spices!